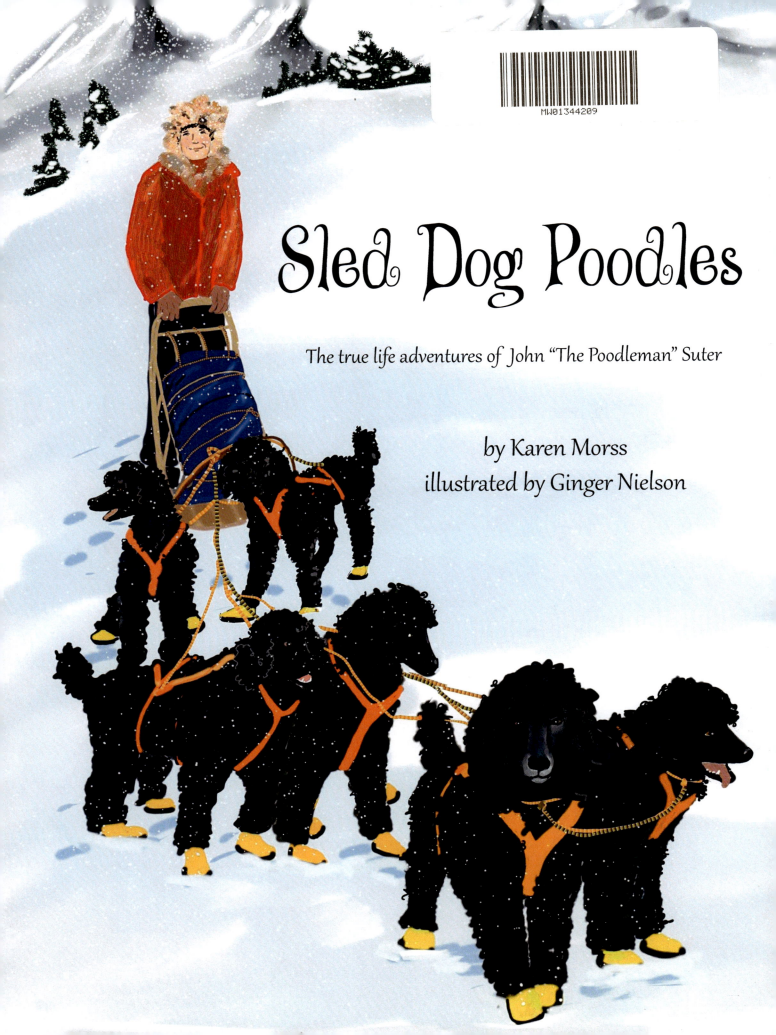

Sled Dog Poodles

The true life adventures of John "The Poodleman" Suter

by Karen Morss
illustrated by Ginger Nielson

A donation will be made on your behalf to Smile Train ~
Saving the world one smile at a time.

Sled Dog Poodles

Special thanks to Rebecca Garner, Nancy Levinson and
John Suter for their help with this story.

Copyright © 2014 Karen Morss and Poodle Dog Productions

This is a work of fiction and no parts of the book or any
illustrations may be used, except in review, without written
permission by Poodle Dog Productions,
775 Upland Road, Redwood City, CA 94062
www.flying-poodles.com

Illustrations copyright © 2014 Ginger Nielson

ISBN-13: 978-1500729134
ISBN-10: 1500729132
Printed in the USA

This Book Belongs To

Dedicated to my father, Hugh Boyd
and Melanie Lynn, my shining lights.   KM

Dedicated my grandfather,
the Reverend Dr. Johannes B. Dahl .   GN

John Suter had a vision that came to him in a dream,
"Run Poodles," spoke Spirit Raven - preposterous it would seem.
But John thought it was a grand idea, as big as big could be,
And dreams are messages straight from the heart, not something to take lightly.

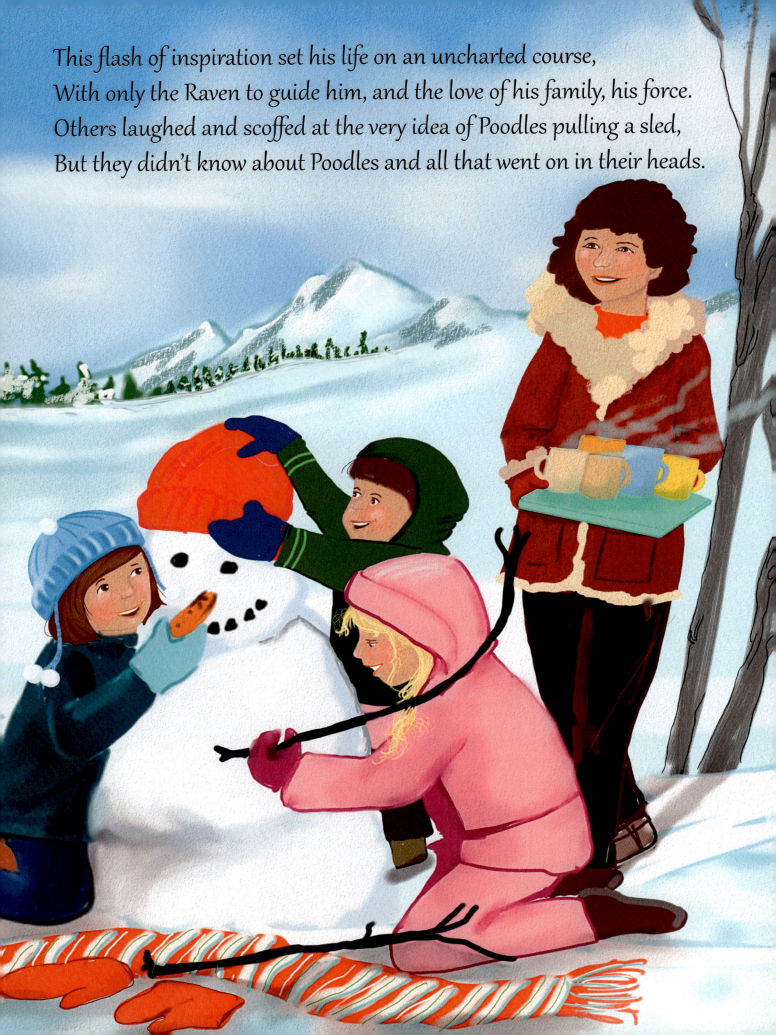

This flash of inspiration set his life on an uncharted course,
With only the Raven to guide him, and the love of his family, his force.
Others laughed and scoffed at the very idea of Poodles pulling a sled,
But they didn't know about Poodles and all that went on in their heads.

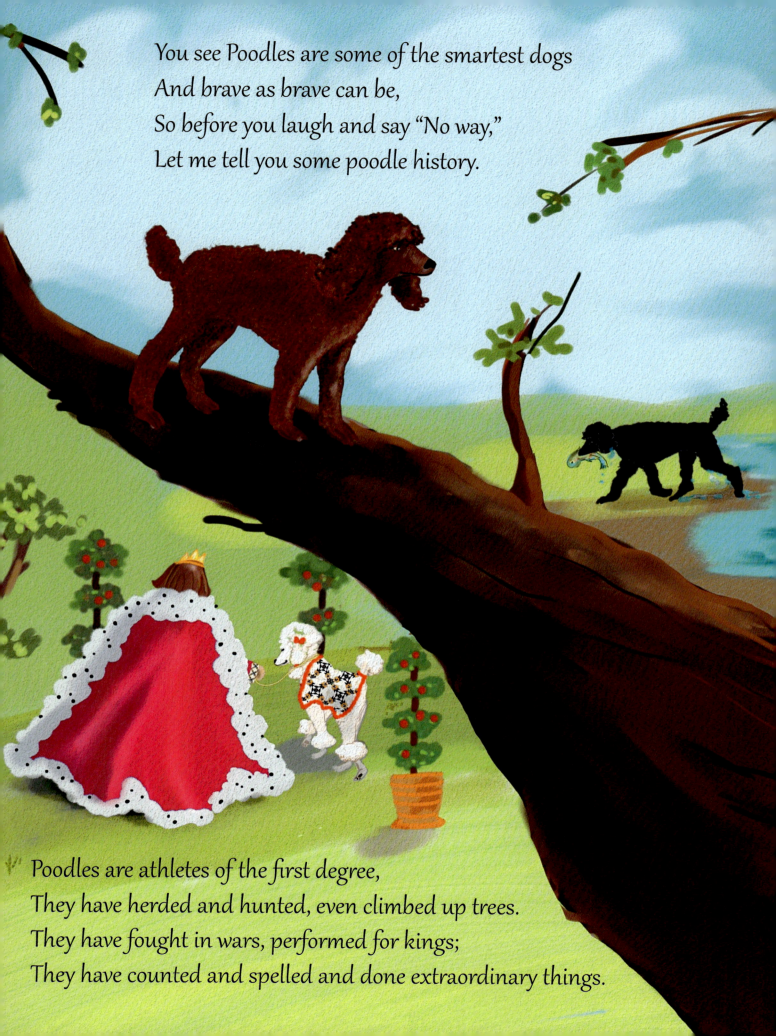

You see Poodles are some of the smartest dogs
And brave as brave can be,
So before you laugh and say "No way,"
Let me tell you some poodle history.

Poodles are athletes of the first degree,
They have herded and hunted, even climbed up trees.
They have fought in wars, performed for kings;
They have counted and spelled and done extraordinary things.

One hundred percent of the experts told John it could not be done,
But he didn't let others define him and he knew that Poodles could run.
John wondered if they could pull a sled and learn to work as a team,
He decided to give them a chance to live the Alaskan Sled Dog dream.

He started with three puppies, two sisters and a boy.
Born of Wycliffe champions, these Standards were no toy.
He named the dogs for villages that dotted the Alaskan state -
Unalakleet, Ninilchik and Knik flew to their home in a crate.

At three months old they were running,
Following John through valleys and hills.
As they grew stronger, they pulled wooden wheels;
They loved these new games and new thrills.

The grass was green those sweet summer days,
They rolled and played in their "poodley" ways;
The runs grew longer but so did their legs,
With John's gentle guidance, no need to beg.

One day they were running by Moose Pass Gas and
What do you think they encountered?
A big Brown Bear stood square in their path.
The brave Poodles kept John surrounded.

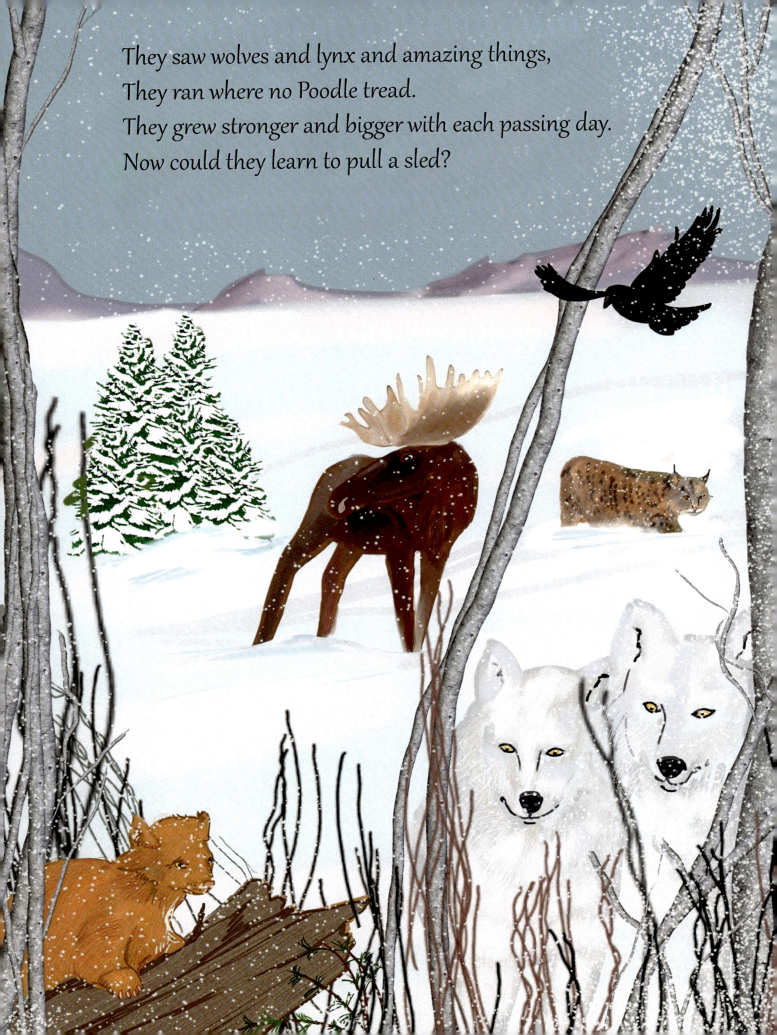

They saw wolves and lynx and amazing things,
They ran where no Poodle tread.
They grew stronger and bigger with each passing day.
Now could they learn to pull a sled?

John built a dogsled, light, fast and strong;
Mary fashioned boots to help them along.
They looked so adorable, it was hard not to gush,
With patience and training, they learned how to mush.

The snow fell gently that first race day;
The Poodles pranced in their "poodley" way.
The children cheered when John gave the shout, "Hike Poodles."
He whistled and the team pulled out.

'Course most people there say "Hey, no way.
The Huskies will eat the Poodles today!"
But a three mile sprint was hardly a run
Considering the training the Poodles had done.

Mary paced back and forth at the finish,
Kept company by her daughters and son.
When all of a sudden the Poodles appeared,
They flew right by and they won!

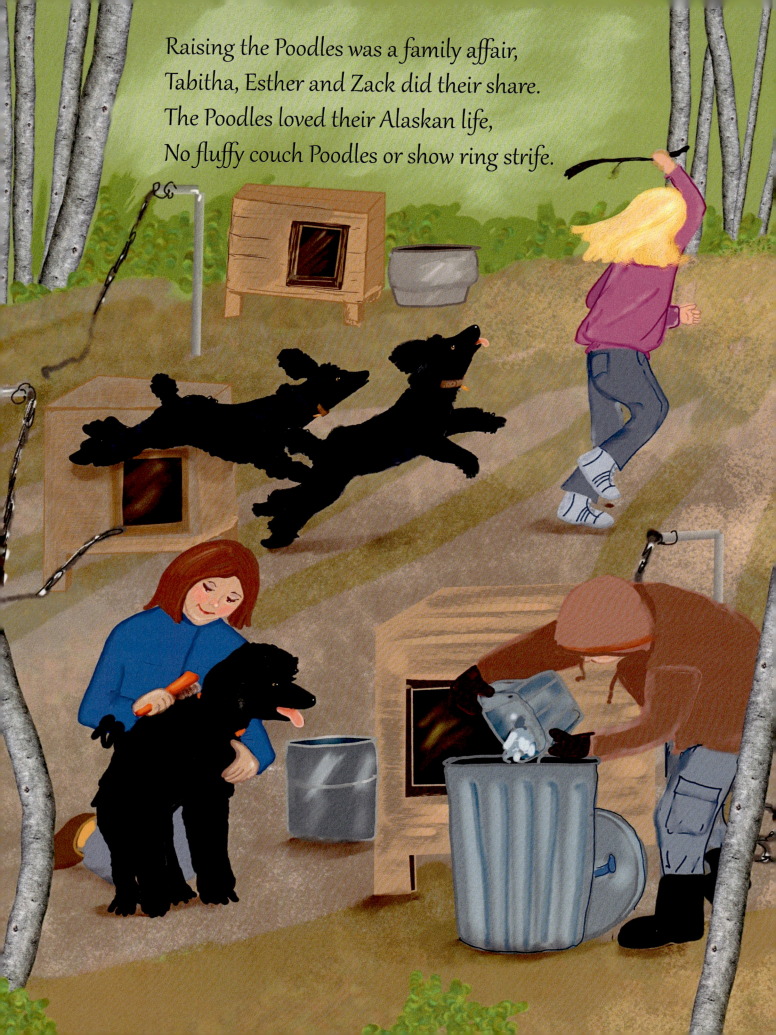

Raising the Poodles was a family affair,
Tabitha, Esther and Zack did their share.
The Poodles loved their Alaskan life,
No fluffy couch Poodles or show ring strife.

They each had a house all snug in the woods,
Knik took up fishing and brought home the goods.
Soon the girls had puppies all wanting to be held
And what was once three, soon became twelve.

John was an athlete of no small repute,
Boxing, judo, and soccer to boot.
So the racing continued and the distances grew,
Now eight Standard Poodles worked as a crew.

He learned many lessons along the way,
Like listening to what each Poodle had to say.
Not every dog was meant to run.
It came from the heart or was not to be done.

But ordinary dreamers live ordinary lives
And John had something much grander in mind -
The Iditarod Trail Sled Dog Race -
And he would not leave the Poodles behind.

It took five generations of Poodles,
Bred and raised the Alaskan way.
The secret to long distance running?
Let the Huskies have their say.

Poodle puppies raised with Huskies
Learn to race as one with the team.
No limits now, with their new sled pals,
Living the Sled Dog Dream.

The distances grew even longer,
Fifty miles was now the new norm.
They met all the rules to enter;
The team was in tiptop form.

All lined up for the start of the race,
Barking dogs all over the place,
Poodle tails up, they started to run,
Just getting here, they'd already won.

One thousand forty nine miles,
From Anchorage to Nome,
Who would believe that Poodles
Could make it all the way home?

Iditarod Map, Southern Route

The Trapline Chatter drummed the story,
The Poodles were on the way.
All the villagers came out to greet them.
"Brave Poodles," the elders say.

The northern lights were a cracklin',
The team ran fast and free,
Then all of sudden, a switchback turn,
John fell off and hit a tree.

Fifi saw what happened
And came to full stop in her track.
Conway, her teammate Husky,
Said "no way, we never go back."

"That's not the way of the Poodle,
We don't leave our family behind,
So get out of my way or help save the day"
And they circled back searching to find.

Righted again they were soon on their way.
Nothing could stop the Poodles that day.
The sled ran fast and so did they.
Great Stars above the Milky Way.

A lone wolf howled while they rested.
At Rainy Pass shelter they find,
Total's foot was hurting.
He would have to stay behind.

They ran and they ran and they ran and they ran
Over mountains, by lakes, in a magic ice land.
When they reached Norton Sound it was blowing real bad,
But the sight in front of them was worse than sad.

Six teams of Huskies lay down in the their tracks.
Wouldn't go forward, wouldn't go back.
John was afraid they all would freeze that night.
"Hike Poodles." He whistled. "It will be all right."

The brave team of Poodles took off at once
And ignored the wind in their face;
They squinted their eyes and ran their best
True Alaskan Sled Dog pace.

As they passed each team just like magic,
The Huskies stood up and ran,
They followed the lead of the Poodles
And they all made it safely to land.

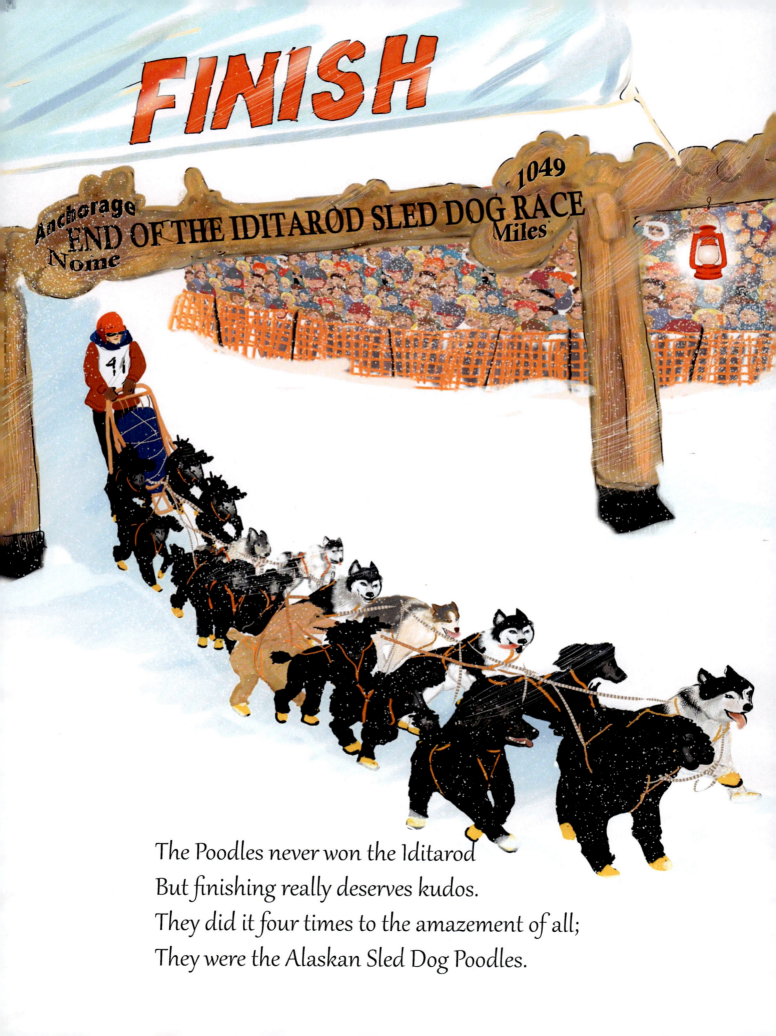

The Poodles never won the Iditarod
But finishing really deserves kudos.
They did it four times to the amazement of all;
They were the Alaskan Sled Dog Poodles.

So if anyone tries to crush your dream,
Just listen to your heart.
Remember the story of the Poodles
Who ran the Iditarod - then just start.

Fun Facts

Musher Talk

Hike	Let's Go	On by	Pass a Team
Haw	Turn Left	Easy	Slow Down
Gee	Turn Right	Whoa	Stop

Dog Sleds are designed for speed.

Dogs wear a special harness, boots, and even coats, when it gets very cold. The coldest temps when the Poodles ran was -70 degrees.

Sled dogs eat about 10,000 calories a day or about five times more than you. They navigate by their sense of smell and prefer to run at night.

Sled Dog Team Positions

The little Red Lantern hangs on the burled arch at the finish line, and remains lit until the last team comes home. John and his team finished 38th out of 52 in 1988.

Forget Me Not
Alaska's State Flower

Check out http://iditarod.com for more information about the race and the Teacher on the Trail program http://itcteacheronthetrail.com
John Suter's website http://home.gci.net/~poodlesleddog/

Made in the USA
San Bernardino, CA
04 January 2019